while we're here
poems | leeza jayde

While We're Here

Copyright © 2021 Leeza Jayde von Alpen.

All rights reserved. No part of this publication may be reproduced, distributed, or transmitted in any form or by any means, including photocopying, recording, or other electronic or mechanical methods, without the prior written permission of the author, except in the case of brief quotations embodied in critical reviews and certain other non-commercial uses permitted by copyright law.

Paperback ISBN: 978-0-6451334-0-0
E-book ISBN: 978-0-6451334-1-7
Hardback ISBN: 978-0-6451334-2-4

Cover design by Nuno Moreira.
Front cover image by Philipp Frohnapfel.
Illustrations by Philipp Frohnapfel.
Water coloured image by Frohnapfel edited by Paige Markland.
Interior design and typography by Laura Jones.

First printing edition 2021.

for Thomas.

you had the most beautiful smile.

I

EPHEMERAL

(EFF-EM-ERR-ALL)
ADJECTIVE

LASTING FOR A VERY BRIEF TIME.
A FLICKER. A BLINK.
A MOMENT

while we're here

home, i've found,
    is not a place.

it is carried
with me
everywhere.

my suitcase full
of hearts, and moments,
and warmth.

— WANDERER

leeza jayde

my journey has taught me
to be gentle
with everyone i meet.

you never know
who has bones,
or who has glass,
sitting quietly
beneath their skin.

— WINEGLASS SKELETONS

while we're here

it's alright if it hurts
to let things go.
this means it was real
and that you have a heart
that works.

— HOW YOU KNOW

leeza jayde

we are all just
wandering souls.
little birds with
b r o k e n wings,
craving for places
we haven't yet flown to,
yearning for nests
we haven't yet built.

— SEARCHING

while we're here

i wake up every morning
and dress myself in metaphors.
i swallow them too quickly
like pills to numb the pain
all just to soften hard truths
because it's so much easier to say
the sun collapsed in my life
than my happiness did.

— PRETTY LIES

leeza jayde

you are more
than what your
memories
whisper to you at 3am.

and you are not a ghost
of all the mistakes
you have ever made.

— MOVING ON

while we're here

       it's okay to hurt.
it's okay if you've kissed
one too many wine bottles
and slumbered beneath
spinning suns.
       it's okay if you've cowered
away from showering
and sunlight and touch
because the warmth
reminds you
of too much
from your past.
       it's okay if you've drowned
in the ebb and flow
of your own thoughts
and only just crawled
your way back to shore.
       it's okay if you've worn tears
like little pearls
and bloody knuckles
like rings
and smiles
like lipstick.
       it's okay if you wandered in the woods.
got lost to find yourself.
if you snapped
paperback spines to be in
any story. *any story*
but your own.

      and it's okay
      if you weren't okay.
because it doesn't matter
that you break.
no.
it only matters
that you grow yourself
back together
and stand comfortable whole
once again.
when you're ready.

and only
when you're ready.

— OKAY

while we're here

before you hold a healing heart
in your eager hands,
look down at them.
ask yourself.
      are they clean?
    are they gentle?
      are they clutching hope?

because what a task it is
to trust again
      after flinching.
but what a gift it is
for someone to invite you
to rest underneath
their aching skin.

— CLEAN YOUR HANDS BEFORE
   YOU HOLD ANOTHER'S

leeza jayde

your experience
does not equate to someone else's.

burn this into your brain.

if you pour the mouthfuls *you* need
into *their* half-empty cup,
this will not necessarily fill it to the brim.

we need to learn to give love
as others need it
not how we
want to receive it.

— EXPECTATIONS

while we're here

AND HERE YOU ARE
walking onwards
DESPITE YOUR BRUISED
and battered
FEET

leeza jayde

i take it,
crumple it into a ball,
and toss it to the salty breeze.
i watch it
drowned and swallowed
beneath the starving waves;
this strange and ridiculous notion
that I AM not ENOUGH.

— ENOUGH
    ALWAYS

while we're here

it's the hearts
who have been badly bruised
that tend to be the ones
which bleed the brightest colours.

— EXPERIENCE

leeza jayde

it's 1am
and i'm watching the waves
wink at me.
they're bathed
in vanilla moonlight
and push and pull,
         push and pull,
the milk of the tide.

it gifts the shore
frothy flotsam
and shells as empty
as his broken promises
and sprays sea salt
like it's mouthwash.

it's 3am and this beating, breathing,
living heart of the earth
glues me to the sand.
it is relentless.
         persistent.
no matter what
jagged rocks
block its waves' path,
it is fluid,
flexible,
swims around it, crashes into it.
smashes through it.

while we're here

and it's 5am now
and i realise that i'm jealous
so strangely jealous
of the ocean
and how it faces
what stands in its way.

— HOW THE SEA MENTORED ME

leeza jayde

while we're here

HOLDING ONTO YOU
was not worth
THE BROKEN FINGERS
the grasping gave
THESE TIRED HANDS.

— A LETTER TO MY GRIEF

leeza jayde

linger in this moment
and lower those raised fists.

how will you ever see
what's in front of you
with a shield of clenched fingers
blotting out your view?

— RELUCTANTLY BRAVE

while we're here

hold them.
that aching soul.
their body buckling forward,
palms splayed, hands raised
in surrender.

hold them.
that lost one
seeking shelter from the storm
buried behind their tender ribs;
from the tempest stirring
beneath their skull.

hold them.
that person staring,
vision blurring,
mouthing *help*
back at you
in your bedroom mirror.

h o l d   t h e m .

— DON'T YOU DARE LET GO

leeza jayde

HOW DO I HEAL EACH TIME?

pass me a pen.

LET ME SHOW YOU

how this works.

while we're here

     i've been that little girl.
the one with broken dreams dripping down
her sleeves.
who has kneeled down in defeat and
breathed out wishes
as strangled whispers
exhaled somewhere between a prayer
and a plead.

     i've been that trusting teenager.
the one with a confidence
that can be measured in grains
pinched between one's thumb and forefinger.
who tried to save the drowning
while she was learning to breathe underwater herself.
who could fix any problems but the ones around
every corner inside the labyrinth of her brain,
buried deep beneath
the ash and soot of her own doubts.

     and i've been that young woman.
the one who filled in the spaces people left as voids
with flowers and other beautiful things.
who learned to love again because her hands
deserved to not flinch away from touch.

leeza jayde

who watered her roots and built herself back up
brick by brick by bloodied brick, from the
marrow outwards.

because that's the thing,
isn't it?

we're all born with this
underrated ability
called breaking

      and healing

and it all depends on what
you choose to focus on.

on where your feet
will carry
you next.

— I WAS. I AM.

while we're here

the truth is that
sometimes our souls
stay up late singing for
a pair of hands
that haven't yet
caressed us.

— YET

leeza jayde

    TAKE YOUR MEDICINE.
drink sunshine,
and swallow laughter.

    TAKE YOUR MEDICINE.
smooth on the soothing balm
of kind words from yourself
to yourself.

    TAKE YOUR MEDICINE.
grasp your demons by the hand.
and whisper to them,
you are only one small black hole
in the forever expanding universe of me.

    ~~TAKE~~ BE YOUR MEDICINE.

— THIS FUNNY THING CALLED HEALING

while we're here

    here's a welcomed grace:

time will slowly,
        ever so slowly,
leach their poison
from your bloodstream,
        and blur the memory
that you never felt
quite enough for them.

— SNAIL'S PACE

leeza jayde

when i was nineteen
i had this useless superpower.

i could feel
alone
in a sea
of people.

unheard
no matter
how much i
raised my
tired voice.

exhausted
no matter
how much sleep
i scrounged.

i had this useless superpower
when i was nineteen.

— WHEN I WAS NINETEEN, PART I

while we're here

build your armour
out of the fragments
life hurtles at you.
but remember
to slip out of it occasionally,
sling it over a chair,
and let the light back in.

leeza jayde

the armour is not your skin.

it is only a shield.

— LET THE LIGHT BACK IN

while we're here

I FALL

like a star

BUT I RISE AGAIN

like the sun

leeza jayde

while we're here

poems,
lingering kisses,
and all of
my heart.

i don't know
who you are yet,
but these will be
my g i f t s
to you.

— ALL I HAVE

leeza jayde

oddly enough,
sometimes
to move forward
we must face
what has been
behind us
all of this time.

— TURN AROUND
    LOOK HOW FAR YOU'VE COME

while we're here

pivot and face your darkness.

now,
       smile.

wave.

strike a match.
       and burn it all down.

— SAY GOODBYE

leeza jayde

gather up your dead roots
in those unsteady hands.
and rip. them. out.

you cannot grow,
you cannot bloom,
if there is rot
eating away at you.

before moving forwards,
you should understand
the journey
you've been through;
how it moulded you.
you are changed
because of it.

you deserve that growth,
but you may have to fight for it.
or you may need to lower your fists.

this is how peace
is often won.
through understanding the enemy.
but that's the thing—

you shouldn't be your own enemy.

while we're here

you are the one person
who will always stay.
until the very end.

you must invest kindness and patience
and long walks with nothing
but your own company
with bigger stretches of time between lovers
in order to get to know yourself better.
you need to do this with your head tilted high,
knee-deep in your thoughts.

you must do
one of the hardest things
you may ever have had, or have, to do.

    you must befriend yourself.

you must befriend yourself to make this journey
a richer one for you.

leeza jayde

so, once again, i ask you
to gather up your dead roots
in those shaking hands
and rip. them. out.

— THE ART OF (INTERNAL) WAR

while we're here

the reality is that
some of us become
artificial flowers
once the love
that flows
through our veins
is staunched.

pain can halt our growth,
scars can stunt our journey.

or you can live by a better truth:

    you are not a flower.

you are a garden
simply waiting
to burst
into full bloom.

— THESE DECISIONS WE MAKE

leeza jayde

ISN'T IT MAGICAL?
HOW WE SPIN G O L D
OUT OF OUR **PAIN.**

while we're here

you are art.
a work in progress.
an interpretive piece.
not everyone will like you
because not everyone
appreciates the same style
and there is nothing wrong with that.

but please
don't settle for being
an oil splatter
when you are, in fact,
an entire painting
of your own making.

— IN CASE NO ONE TOLD YOU TODAY

leeza jayde

depression
is having
a coldness settle
underneath your skin,
while others tell you
how warm the sunshine
feels again today.

while we're here

this is why it is important,
so deeply important,
to reach within
and thaw someone
from the inside
out.

— ALL THIS LIGHT
        AND I CANNOT TOUCH IT

leeza jayde

i was icarus.

staring into you
seared my eyes,
burning an image
too bright
to be truly warm.
you left me blinking,
staining eddies of oily light
into my wide eyes.

you were the sun,
the scorching cold light
of the sun,

and i was icarus
flying straight
into you.

— I KNOW HOW THIS STORY ENDS

while we're here

I TURNED

my misery into

MY MUSE,

and suddenly

EVERYONE STARTED

calling me

A POET

what broke me
was not that you left.

it was that you couldn't bear
to stay.

— NOT A POEM

while we're here

i try to shine
a light on my demons
but they love
the attention.

— LIMELIGHT

leeza jayde

why doesn't
this house
feel like
a home?

— THIS SKIN I LIVE IN

while we're here

love made me a soldier.
and when it died,
i slept with the lights on.

none of my clothes fit after two weeks
and i forgot what i sounded like after three.
i bended my knees so often in prayer
that they were perpetually bruised.
i consumed books like i was starving,
then i got drunk, so desperately drunk,
on the syllables of poets
who knew better than me
of what it meant to heal.

and i learned to be gentle
so very gentle
with myself
because you must handle
all fragile things with care.

and yet, even so, rain passed through my eyes
still far too often and sometimes
it felt like the season would never

        never.
              never.

change.

leeza jayde

and i was tired. so damn tired
that even sleep would not alleviate
the blue-black memories
sagging beneath my eyes.

but now i am stronger.
my shoulders are iron
and my tongue is silver.
i can speak honey
to the suffering
because i am fluent
in their language.

and if i have
learned anything,
it is this:

you will still quake.
your knees will still buckle.
your eyes will still flood.

because even a tree's leaves must fall
before it blooms again in spring.

— TO HEAL IS TO HURT ALONG THE WAY

while we're here

do not mourn those not dead;
feel their absence,
but do not walk with ghosts.

do not drown in
that warm liqueur of memories,
as tempting as it is.

— LET THE PRESENT SOBER YOU

leeza jayde

    be.

    be a lighthouse in the storm.
use the lessons time has gifted you to guide others
away from the jagged rocks they cannot see
while they're losing their grip steering.
    be a lighthouse in the storm.

    be a kind mouth.
ensure every syllable you speak
drips with compassion
and either grounds or lifts others up,
and nothing less.
    be a kind mouth.

    be patient hands.
stop sneaking glances at your watch,
restlessly waiting for you
to hurry up and heal.
    be patient hands.

    be all the good
that lives in the
nooks and crannies
of this fractured world.
    be all the good.

— BE

while we're here

suffering should not be romanticised.
       but it is.

it is not a dying fire or gentle weeping
through long lashes or strained smiles
or longing sighs like the spring breeze.

it is a match licking your exposed wrist,
catching alight, and burning without remorse,
crippling your grip on reality.
it's showerless weeks and starving stomachs
rejecting meals and permanently curved spines
from too many hours spent bowing your head
between your knees, palms pressed
to your temples chanting *please stop*

    please stop

please stop
       why won't you just stop?

it is not recognising the cries your lips howl
in the dead of night.
it is recoiling from concerned hands.
it is masquerading smiles to avoid

questions you do not wish to answer,

and simple conversations that cost energy
you no longer possess.

suffering should not be romanticised.
sad girls and sad boys being sad
should not be romanticised.

there is nothing beautiful about it.

> but do you know what is beautiful?
> what poetry and song lyrics and movies
> should all
> turn their attention to
> instead of this false, glorified silhouette imagery?

it's wisdom.
the wisdom sleeping in your scars today.
when the night has set and the sun has risen,
and life is breathed back into your dry bones,
you can appreciate the aftermath.
    the healing.
how strong you were to walk on coals
and crawl with shattered shins,
dragging splintered bones in the dark
the long way home,
and yet still
        still
you learned to walk again.

every new crack in your skin is flooded with gold.
you are a teacher now. relatable. raw. real.

while we're here

japanese artisans innovated an artform
that praises this.
how things some eyes might perceive as broken
are still priceless in another's perception;

where fissured veins in pottery
are coloured in with lacquered gold
to emphasise the value of experience.

kintsugi art, they called it. yes.

    art.

    what a wonderful word.

kintsugi, then, is this tangible manifestation
of perseverance. strength. courage.

and that's you.

    that's *you.*

you and your
    kintsugi skin.

— THAT'S YOU

leeza jayde

i crave the taste
of simpler times.

— FAMISHED

while we're here

i'm too hard on myself.

i blame myself when all my little pieces
don't fit into puzzles with pretty pictures.

because it's painful
to have spent so much time,
invested so much heart,
only to lose it.
and i get so caught up
in temporary things like heartache
that i forget how i gained something
much more valuable.

memories.
lessons learned.
imprints.

evidence
that i was not afraid to live
while i was alive.
proof
that i was here and i was brave and i tried.
      that i was *here*.

and i can't blame myself for that.

— I REGRET NOTHING

leeza jayde

the fact that our skin sheds
means it instinctively welcomes the future,
and releases the past.

your body is naturally protective of you.
it will unconsciously coat you
in an entirely new shield of cells.
skin they never touched.

so do not cling onto it. them.
what-ifs and has-beens.
you are halting your growth.

once butterflies wiggle free from their chrysalis
they never look back.

— HOW MUCH OUR BODIES LOVE US,
EVEN WHEN WE DON'T

while we're here

THE RIGHT ONES
WON'T TELL YOU TO
thicken your skin.

THEY WILL SLIP
UNDERNEATH IT
and join you.

leeza jayde

hearts are like paper.
aren't they?

time has folded each of us
into different sculptures.

the older we get,
the more we crease.
and i think that's magical.

— ORIGAMI HEARTS

while we're here

please don't apologise
for flinching when you've been bruised.

    just don't.

don't you ever apologise
for being raw and real and untamed.

    don't.
don't you ever apologise
for being ice some days
and water on others.

    don't.
don't you ever apologise
for your scars.
for your healing.
for your wild.
    don't.

leeza jayde

apologies are for when we've wronged someone.
not for when we've been true to ourselves
and it just so happens to not correlate
with what others want.

there's no need for you to apologise
for taking up space.
       for using the mouth you were given.
for not smiling all the time.
       for not healing quickly.
for not bending your branches
to the will of another's wind.
       for not being leashed or told.
for wanting respect and love and a safe place to grow.
       for saying *no* when they want *yes*.
for needing space from noise and social rendezvous.
       for falling. for rising. for falling again.

don't ever apologise for these things.
       because you don't need to.

and the ones who are worth it, who truly support you
and care for your wellbeing will respect this.

— A GENTLE REMINDER

while we're here

truly. it was something beautiful.
how you gently loved
these little broken bones.

— MY MOTHER

leeza jayde

when i was born,
you swaddled me in book pages.
you read to me while i cooed in my crib
of worlds where queens toppled
crooked kingdoms,
where women wielded swords and a girl could be
the smartest person in the room.

when i turned six,
you put a pen in my hand and told me to write
and to never stop writing, and that if i did,
it would deprive the world of something
it desperately needs.

and when i had that stroke during my college years,
i know it killed you to see me struggle
to stitch together even simple syllables
about how my day went
because that is something you never wanted for me:
    to be silenced in a world
where not everyone wants me to speak up.

i take after your love of writing, you see,
and so, i sincerely hope you know that
without you,
there wouldn't be any words
at all.

— MY FATHER

while we're here

DON'T BELIEVE
in 'truths'
FROM THE LIPS.
only from the heart
AND FINGERTIPS.

leeza jayde

i have spent far too long
looking for love in places
where it does not exist.

in stranger's compliments
and attention boys gave me
when i traded my hand-me-down softball shorts
for skinny jeans that showed my thigh gap
at fifteen.
in working myself to the bone
for the approval of my peers
to be the very best, without rest,
without peace, without sleep,
until my brain shut down
and i had to learn to speak again
at twenty-one.

in baggy sweaters to hide
how my skeleton poked through
my tightened skin
because i was told i looked pretty
when i was hungry
and to be pretty was to be respected—
        wasn't it?

while we're here

in a boy in a man's body
who tried and failed to understand trauma
and shamed me for it, blamed me for it,
left me for her for it

because she was normal and i was damaged.
and because he wanted all my light
without wanting to understand my darkness too.

i have searched for love in places
where it does not exist.
confused it for attention and applause and accolades
and lived my life with a black eye
when i should have looked in the mirror,
held my own hand,
left longer gaps between loves
and learned where it *does* live.

in me
and in everything i have yet to offer.

— 3AM AWAKENINGS

leeza jayde

WE
have all these
MOUTHFULS OF *MAYBE*S,
and bulging pocketfuls
OF *TOMORROW*S,
but I believe
IN LIVING
n o w

.

.

.

BEFORE YOU NOTICE
that your internal clocks
HAVE WOUND DOWN
and suddenly
YOU NO LONGER
possess the
TIME.

while we're here

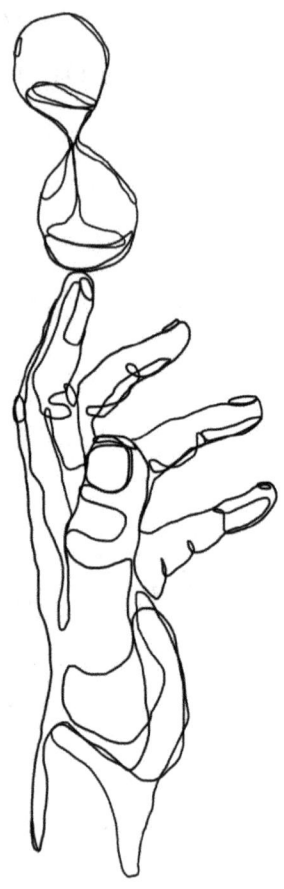

leeza jayde

HEARTS, YOU SEE, HAVE THIS RATHER INCONVENIENT CAPACITY TO BREAK—

but they also tend to become reshaped
in the wake of their breakage; to be smelted,
after cracking, and be forged through time and
pain into something *softer* (but stronger) than it
ever was before.

but you must let your heart be molded in this way.
you must invite the kintsugi. it will not just barge in.
and to let it flow through your cracks and wash out
your nicks and cuts from battle,
you need to accept this difficult truth:

sometimes, we need to wander in waves
too deep for us, so that we might better learn
how to swim.

sometimes, we need to stumble through bitter nights
to best appreciate the warmth of the dawn.

sometimes, we will feel pain even though we did
not deserve it. and, often, we'll need to forgive
ourselves when we don't think that we necessarily
should.

while we're here

pain is deeply uncomfortable, unwanted, exhausting.
but it is an inextricable part of exisisting.

IT SHAPES US ALL UNIQUELY.

some become hardened, others husks,
and others further still become gentle,
and sensitive, to other people's suffering.
there are invaluable teachings to be learned,
regardless of the outcome.

but we all have one thing in common,
despite our disparities:

we have suffered.

    and we survived.

AND ONCE YOU SURVIVE, YOU CAN HEAL.

but you cannot rebuild
until the wreckage has been cleared away;
you cannot restore what was burned
until the ash that settled over your skin
has been swept aside.

SO PICK UP YOUR BROOM,
    and take a deep breath.

leeza jayde

there is a lot of work to be done in turning smoke back to flesh. and all that grey coiling up inside of you won't sigh itself away.

II

RESILIENCE
(REZ-ILL-EE-NSS)
NOUN

THE CAPACITY TO RECOVER FROM ADVERSE
CIRCUMSTANCES OR OBSTACLES.
PERSEVERANCE. ADAPTABILITY.
RESISTANCE.

leeza jayde

FIERCE

raw

WOUNDED

—but still here

THAT'S WHO YOU

really are.

while we're here

fierce. raw. wounded.
but still here.
that's who you
really are.

not every tear or stifled cry.
not the breaking or slow healing.
not all the wounded things you hissed
when you were backed into a corner.

      no.

it is human to hurt.
but do not let memories
of yesterday
define you
today.

it takes a special kind of
      strength
to keep walking
with broken bones.

to learn from lessons
that both broke and rebirthed you.

leeza jayde

your super power is that you
still get up. still show up. still try.
    still have hope.

you chose these decisions.
even when your mind was messy.
even when it tested you.
even when you thought you had nothing left
in the tank.

and i think that makes you very,
very courageous indeed.

while we're here

so here's to you and your strength,
because that's who you really are.

not weak, but human.

not broken, but healing.

not a failure, but a learner.

resilient.

i like that word.

      resilient.

— DECISIONS

leeza jayde

i found someone
strong enough
to help me carry
all of these heavy memories.

    it's me.

— IT ALWAYS HAS BEEN

while we're here

AND WHEN THE RAINS CAME

i learned to dance on water

AND WHEN THE WAVES CRASHED
AGAINST MY SKIN

i learned to love the taste of salt

AND WHEN MY WORLD FLOODED

i learned to see the beauty of the deep

leeza jayde

let me tell you something.

it was me who held a torch against my shadows.

i reached behind these ribs
and challenged my heart.

i coloured my soul back in
after they bleached my bones.

and *i* was the one who taught myself
this foreign language
called smiling
and meaning it.

so let's be really clear here:

i never needed him to be my hero.

    i *am* the hero.

— STOP STANDING ON MY CAPE,
   AND GET OUT OF MY WAY

      I HAVE A CITY TO SAVE

while we're here

i fought
for the little girl
who i was,
and for who she
wanted me to be.

and i know
she would applaud me
for who i have become.

— HAPPIER

some things are bigger than love.

your health. your space. your dreams.
your sanity. your peace. your comfort.
your quiet. your stability. your here and now.

you.
you are bigger, more important, than the way
someone makes you feel.
especially if you are coming last,
simply slotting into the cracks
of a relationship with someone
who is crumbling you
and everything you built
or wish to yet build.

if any of the above things are being ignored
or disregarded,
please gift yourself enough kindness
to leave.

— WAVE A WHITE FLAG AND WALK AWAY

while we're here

some days
i am diamonds
and some days
i am glass.

— AND THAT IS OKAY

THAT IS OKAY

leeza jayde

fellow musician,
it's okay to feel off-key;
a symphony of sound
will often have
rolling thunder,
and crying keys
before that slow,
warm melody
returns and echoes
in your heart
once more.

— YOU CAN'T RUSH A SLOW TEMPO

while we're here

you thought you'd
scraped me clean,
like an empty cantaloupe.
but then, just when
i thought that i had nothing
left to give,
the sun rose
and i blossomed fruit
once again.

— YOU WERE MISTAKEN

leeza jayde

stop demanding that you grow so quickly.

you wouldn't plant seeds
only to dig them up again
and see how strong the roots are.
       to see how much you've grown.

my love, don't you know,
that gardening
doesn't work that way?

— BE PATIENT WITH YOUR IMPATIENCE

while we're here

darling.
your worth
cannot be measured
by all those hands
who weren't ready
to hold you.

your own hands
are the only measuring cups
that you will ever need.

— MEASURING CUPS

leeza jayde

one day, i woke up
and realised that
i'd given him
all my love,
all my time,
all this poetry,
and kept none of it
for myself.

— IT IS NO WONDER
    THAT I FELT SO EMPTY

while we're here

please.

please don't farewell
your softness,
because you went
through hard times.

there are too many
harsh words,
and swinging fists
in this world already.

we need all the softness
that we can get.

— PLEASE

leeza jayde

people will
shed their layers
for a gentle sun
more than they will
for bitter rain.

— IT'S SIMPLE

        BE KIND

while we're here

learning to smile again,
and smile sincerely,
is more difficult
than you might imagine.

but it is not
impossible.

it is simply
an old language
returning to
your lips.

— MUSCLE MEMORY

leeza jayde

the thing is,
you can't expect
yourself to stand tall
if the weight of
the solar system is weighing
on your shoulders.

— GIFT YOURSELF SOME WELL-DESERVED REST

while we're here

there will be
so many days
when you'll be
the kind of tired
that sleep simply
cannot fix.

— WHAT THEY DON'T TELL YOU ABOUT
THIS PROCESS

leeza jayde

and the realisation came unannounced to me
    late one early morning.
it budded in my mind
like a seed stretching up through its topsoil;
a whisper of a thought
    at last beginning to take root.

that's when a flower started growing
        in my brain.

'you have spent so long waiting for that someone,
instead of working on yourself,' it said.
'you're waiting for a pair of palms cupping a glue gun
and band-aids, when what you really need

        is a watering can.

        and you can do that,' it told me.
        'nobody else should do it for you.

        you can do that.

        you can hold
            a watering can.'

        — WATERING CANS

while we're here

it has dawned on me over time
that it's okay to break down.

even the brightest star
must collapse before
it can be born anew,
like a phoenix
from the flame.

so let yourself crumble.

it is not a sign of weakness.
it is your humanity shining through.
and tears alone cannot douse
that deeply pitted fire
forever flaring within you.

— RISE FROM THE ASHES. AS MANY TIMES AS IT TAKES.

leeza jayde

look for the heart
of every storm,
where the winds
are at their quietest,
and breathe *that* in.

do this, and i promise,
you can survive
whatever debris
the weather
whips you with.

— A REALISTIC OPTIMIST

while we're here

I AM BROKEN
don't tell me that
I AM HEALING

I AM WEAK
don't tell me that
I AM STRONG

I AM EMPTY
don't tell me that
MY HEART IS SLOWLY FILLING

— NOW READ THIS POEM IN REVERSE

leeza jayde

oh, but i am in
f r a g m e n t s .

i hope that you
love puzzles.

— JUST FOR NOW

while we're here

an ingredient list
        for healing:

    one spoonful
of willingness
to learn the language
of appreciation.

    a pinch
of grit teeth
through the challenge
of acceptance
with what has happened
before today.

    and one handful of your beating heart
ready to invite forgiveness,
and to reject
the wolves within.

— CUT OUT AND KEEP THIS RECIPE

leeza jayde

embrace the grief,
and then embrace
your capacity to repair
the galaxies
inside of you.

— YOU WERE DESIGNED TO HEAL

while we're here

time gently held my hands, and stroked them.
it leaned forward, quietly murmuring in my ear,
    'it's a lie, you know.
        what they tell you about me, i mean.'

i bristled then, demanding to know what that meant.

'i can't heal all wounds. i can't heal *you*,' it told me.

and i suddenly felt so desperately lost.
    because if time cannot do this,
        then what will?

'i cannot heal you,' time repeated,
    'not unless,' it added, and i looked up,
    'you let me.'

leeza jayde

i really looked at time then,
in a way i never really had before,
and it stared back, and whispered
something i never forgot.

'you know,' time smiled at me,
'my deepest hope for you
is that i opened your eyes,

and now
well
you simply
cannot close them.'

— CONVERSATIONS WITH MY CLOCK

i'm frequently picking fights
with my past.
and you know what?

i always lose.

— CHOOSE YOUR BATTLES

leeza jayde

i refuse for my
quality of life
to be compromised
because of past hurt
that i never asked
to have happen to me.

— I DESERVED BETTER,

    SO I'LL GIFT BETTER TO MYSELF

while we're here

let the pain
envelope you.
let it wash out
your weary eyes,
and help you see
the world anew.

do not let your pain
go to waste.

it is a messenger.
a lesson.

learn from it.

— RENEWAL

leeza jayde

if it seems like
you have so much further
to go in your journey,
then stop.
       turn around.

take a look. really look
and appreciate
how far you've already come.

one day felt like it would never end,
but it became a week.
one week felt impossible to crawl through,
but it became a month.

time never stopped.

you never stopped.

that's a testament to you
and your might.

now, i ask you again,
to stop. to look.
to appreciate
how far you've come.

— THESE ROADS WE'VE TRAVELLED

while we're here

you know

EVEN AT OUR BEST

we are all still

SO FLAWED

leeza jayde

i am so tired of living in a world full of crow eyes.

we reside in a society obsessed
    with shiny things.

with flawless, poreless, unrealistic expectations.
then we claw at each other's throats to get it. to feel it.
    to be it.

we are not animals.
    but we act like it.

but lust doesn't last.
    lust is temporary. impulsive. empty.

that desire, that thirst,
    can never be completely quenched.
it's a dying throat drinking seawater.
never satisfied for long.
    the flesh is temporarily sated.
our stomachs are content. but they are not full.

because the mind, the heart, the soul,
    are still hollow. there is no substance.

while we're here

to fill yourself, to quench that thirst,
you need milk and honey. substance.
from the kind syllables only caring lips can pour.
it doesn't come from fingertips that excitedly explore.

it can be found hiding in the heart
during past-our-bedtimes conversations,
not a quickened pulse that flares to life
when we see exposed skin.

here, then, is how to feel full.

      pry out your crow eyes.
purge the seawater from your lungs.

look for what will sustain you.

seek a meal. not a snack.

living on bowls of sugar and syrup
will not carry you forward.

      no.

so
    here's where you'll find real beauty. substance.

leeza jayde

look for the way eyes smile and glitter
when people talk about why they get out of bed.

how people sacrifice their only time here
and energy to build ladders for those
who can't quite make the climb alone.

the way voices hitch, and breath is lost,
when people trust you with what it meant
to lose their way. themselves. stray.
and what all this pain taught them, because pain
is valuable, and people are incredible
for going through it.

how hands tremble when they talk about
that God left them.
how they surrender and reach skyward
when they understand that
      He never really left.

while we're here

that.
> that's beauty.

and i want to find it between all these crow eyes.

> i don't want shiny.

i don't want temporary. empty. unfulfilling.

i want substance.

> i want something real.

— I WANT TO FEEL FULL

leeza jayde

your magic is that
you can still
s m i l e
after all that you
have been through.

— YOUR MAGIC

while we're here

you may be lost,
and found,
a thousand times
before you
truly know yourself.

but, once you do,
you're going to meet
someone very special indeed.

— THE FINDING

i was not afraid
of losing you.
i was afraid
of losing myself
in the pieces
that i gave to you.
and i have found
so many more
where that came from
since you left.

— SO MANY MORE

while we're here

i am learning
this odd
and new thing
called loving
m y s e l f .

— HELLO,
    IT'S NICE TO MEET YOU

leeza jayde

YOU ARE A MOST BEAUTIFUL COLLECTION OF ATOMS.

the universe has strung you together so deliberately
to form a human being with a heart capable of loving,
a mind capable of learning, and hands capable of holding,
that it is hard to believe that your existing is in any way
an accident. i refuse to believe that.

YOUR VERY BEING WAS MADE TO LAUGH.

this is why children, when given the opportunity,
  will smile
so naturally. because before we learn pain, our
  primal state involves joy.

YOUR BODY WAS DESIGNED FOR SURVIVAL.

it is your body's natural order of things to heal you;
when you bleed, our body fights to weave cells together
to cease the flow. our tongues are the fastest healing organs
in the body—and the strongest. you were created to
  speak up.
our hands instinctively curl into fists when we
  are angered,
because the body knows it deserves a fighting chance.
and you need to give that to yourself—
                             a fighting chance.

while we're here

SO BE KIND TO YOURSELF. GIVE BACK TO YOURSELF.

help your mind to heal by not self-sabotaging your happiness in choosing to live with old ghosts.
exorcise them instead.
heal yourself, and let others
help you through your journey.
allow yourself to be bold, be bright, be passionate.
                            be entirely yourself.

you'll have so many stories to tell at the end.

REMEMBER—
    YOU ARE A MOST BEAUTIFUL COLLECTION OF ATOMS.

so be whole with your chemistry.

       be whole.

III

EPIPHANY

(EE-PIFF-AH-NEE)
NOUN

A MOMENT IN TIME WHEN ONE EXPERIENCES
AN ABRUPT AND SIGNIFICANT REVELATION
OR UNDERSTANDING OF SOMETHING.
A DAWNING.
    AN AWAKENING.

leeza jayde

i am learning
to appreciate all of
the little things
in life,

including
myself.

— IT'S A JOURNEY

if you want to hold another person's pieces,
then you need to be willing to give
pieces of yourself in return.
i have learned this the hard way.

this can be daunting when you've tried before,
and someone stole them from you,
then walked away, slamming
your outstretched fingers in the door.

but not everyone is like that.
and you'll never find them
    if you don't give.

it's normal to be scared if all you've known is thieves.

you should, of course, keep the best parts of you
for yourself. only share them. don't gift them away.

deep love is not selfish.
but it is not necessarily selfless either.
    it is balanced.

and that's the thing.
you need to be willing to take a leap of faith.
you need to be willing to try.

— TRY

leeza jayde

if you are told that you are loved,
believe them when they say it
w i t h o u t   w o r d s .

love lies in the
delivery of actions,
and not the husks
of empty syllables.

— ACTIONS MOVE MOUNTAINS

while we're here

your seasoned hands
have always guided
my tentative ones.

you held my little fingers
as i learned to walk, lifted me when
i fell. and i've fallen many times
in my life since learning to crawl.
still do. it's the human in me.
and, yet, your hands were ever patient.
ever gentle. ever *with* me.

you taught me to stick my fingers
in the clouds and swirl,
to cradle stars and stain my eyelids with them.

to clutch roots where others favour flowers
and appreciate what growth means.

leeza jayde

your fingers have always grasped,
released, sacrificed
so much for me.
never gestured for much in return.

those same hands dried my eyes,
cupped the back of my neck
and held me to the crook of yours
when breathing felt like bleeding.

those same hands hold mine now
and your eyes crease and i realise
that despite everything
i would do *anything*
to keep your hands this soft,
just as you have done everything
so that i could know what it is
to hold dreams in the palm of my hands,
to bring them to my lips and sip.
that nothing is ever truly out of my reach

so long as i stretch for it.

while we're here

and it's dawning on me now
as i laugh at it over lunch with you
while you reach across the table
and squeeze my knuckles.

there really is nothing
quite like
my mother's hands.

— YOUR HANDS

leeza jayde

there are so many f l a v o u r s
in this lifetime.
      and i want to taste it all.
the sweet, the zesty
      —even the bitter.
so that when i am eventually lowered
into the earth's cradle,
i can know that there was not one feeling
that i did not appreciate the palate of.

i will know that i had *the* human experience,
in all its wonder, in all its pain.
for we do not truly appreciate sweetness
until we too have savoured the sour.

and then, in the end,
only after all of these flavours,
and only then,
will i feel what it is like
for a soul to have been well-fed.

— THE HUMAN EXPERIENCE

while we're here

we idolise
the untouched ones,
but it's the practiced hearts
that know how to
take care of you
the most,
for they have had
more practice,
more pain,
more *more*.

i am not secondhand.

i am simply well-learned
in how to sink,
or swim,
in this river
we all want to drink from,
label love,
and gently drown in.

— MORE

leeza jayde

let's build a hearth
with all of the
sticks and stones
that ever broke
your bones.

i'll help you burn them all down,
and then we'll warm our hands
over the rising flames.

— A BONFIRE FOR BAD MEMORIES

while we're here

there might come a time
where
m e m o r i e s
are all that you have.

so i sincerely hope
that you collect
ones that are bright
and beautiful enough
to keep you warm at night.

—— WILL THE RECOLLECTIONS YOU COLLECTED

BE ENOUGH?

leeza jayde

i have found that
love is like the sea.

its waves can often

push
         and
   pull

      at you.

there is no reasoning with it.
no map or compass or oar
that can guide, or steer, you
either forward, or backward,
towards the safety of the shore.

and then there's me.

  the sailor
who still doesn't know
   how to swim.

—— PUSH AND PULL, PUSH AND PULL

while we're here

    so here's the truth.

i wasn't looking for love
    when it walked up to me
one summer night
    in a crowded room.

and it scared
    the hell out of me
how much i liked
    how it sounded
when it whispered to me.

the way it asked
    for my name.

—— FEBRUARY 22ND, 2019, 10:59PM

leeza jayde

you slowly breathe out my name
like you're stretching out taffy
and i have to ask,

does the word taste
as honeyed
as it sounds
on your tongue?

— QUESTIONS THAT KEEP ME AWAKE

while we're here

a sea of hands,
but only your fingers
can intertwine with mine
so fluidly.

— BUT I'M NOT SURE IF I CAN SWIM

WITH ALL THESE BROKEN BONES

leeza jayde

I FELL THROUGH

the ocean

AND INTO

your arms.

while we're here

and, just like that,
you woke this
sleeping heart of mine.

— RESUSCITATION

leeza jayde

there's a symphony
rising, and rolling,
in my chest
just for you.

— AND IT TERRIFIES ME

while we're here

    how will i know
when i'm ready?

    how do i love without hearing old voices
scraping the inside of my skull?

    how do i fan these flames without
burning you to the ground?

    how do i fall
without a parachute to help me land?

    how do i love both you and myself
and not get lost this time?

— I DON'T KNOW
    IF I CAN DO THIS AGAIN

leeza jayde

my tongue cannot keep up
with the pace of my heart
when you're around.

and i'm left here,
stumbling over syllables.
grasping for them
and finding nothing.

because you both bring the words
and steal them away.

so here i am.

a writer
without any words
at all.

— FUMBLING

while we're here

maybe, just maybe,

not everyone is like
everyone i've ever known.

leeza jayde

and maybe, just maybe,
i need to practice
what i preach.

— TO LIVE WHILE I'M ALIVE

while we're here

it is hard work,
this chipping away at these stone walls.
this opening of locked doors.

    this letting you in.

— I'LL LEAVE THE KEY UNDER THE MAT FOR YOU

leeza jayde

falling.
it sounds like fear.
so i think, perhaps,
that i did not fall for you.

     no.

because loving you
doesn't feel like falling.

     it feels like coming home.

it feels like light. handfuls of it
that caress my ears, warming me,
when you speak.

it feels like whispered kindness,
and cold fire when our lips collide,
and like i've swallowed a sunrise in winter
     when you stare at me like that.

it's sighing into your arms after a long day.
it's a crescendo rising in my throat,
and bright symbols crashing,
and the ocean bathing, cleansing, the cuts in my skin.
     it's a star exploding behind my chest

while we're here

when you gently help my grandmother down stairs,
or smile at the woman who raised me,
or ask me how my day unfolded.
it feels like moments i'll pocket
and burn forever behind my eyelids.

like bandaged knees, and bedtime stories,
fresh socks in thunderstorms, nightlights,
and balms to old bruises.

it's an answered prayer.
       a renewed hope.

so perhaps i did not fall.

perhaps i just came home.
to a pair of smiling eyes who gave me a story
       and listened to mine.

and i think that's what love is.

the stories we share.

the chapters we write
      together

      with the right ones.

— WHAT LOVE IS

while we're here

you're my 1am thoughts.
the spaces between
my fingers.
the laughter that lives
on the tip of my tongue now.
eyepiece. umbrella. shield.
sugar in my tea.

i'm a wanderer and you're woodlands.
a summer thunderstorm
quenching the drought
in this arid, dusty sea of red earth.

because that's the thing.

without meaning to,
you've become my favourite things about breathing
when my lungs feel like giving out.

— WITHOUT MEANING TO

leeza jayde

YOU MAKE

THE **PLANETS**

IN ME

S P I N

while we're here

some mornings
i raise my fingertips to my eyelids
and realise that
they are wide open.
my lashes wet
with glittering stars.

in those heartbeats,
i remember
that the universe of us
is not a dream.

all that time
my younger self spent
scrawling words into a battered journal
filled with quiet whispers
that i bled through my pen then,
staining those pallid pages
with prayers
for another soul who looked up
and saw more than just the sky.

leeza jayde

and it feels like
every footstep,
every bruise,
every poem
led to here. to now.
      to us.
to this quiet room.
and your gentle hands
brushing mine.

to these vanished syllables
i can't quite grip
to utter my gratitude
for the miracle of you.

because the truth is
all you need to do
is look at me
with those dark-rimmed eyes
and suddenly
i've swallowed the universe.

and you,
only you,
can make the planets in me
spin.

— I'M AN ASTRONAUT AT HEART

while we're here

peel back your armour
and let this fresh mountain air
mend your heart.

— YOU HIKED SUMMITS ON THIS JOURNEY

                        NOW TAKE IN THE VIEW

leeza jayde

love after trauma
is the prying back
of one's ribs,
to expose a tattered organ,
and trusting someone
to handle it
g e n t l y .

— VULNERABLE. RAW.

while we're here

like a flower
opening its face
to the sun,
you make the
caution tape
around my heart
u n f u r l.

— LIKE A FLOWER

i have read
a thousand stories,
and ours will always be
my favourite.

while we're here

LIKE THE

SAND AND SEA

we

COLLIDED.

leeza jayde

those voices in your head may speak up once in a while.
because the louder they are, the longer they'll take to die.
    but all things have a lifespan—even pain.

it's not about banishing them with sheer willpower.
for most people, it cannot be done this way.

pulling weeds from a garden takes time.
and effort. and sometimes,
when those unwanted seedlings
start to sprout again, you will realise
that you missed a part of your garden
that needed more nurturing than you thought it did.
    and that's alright.

growing is about letting yourself make these mistakes,
and it's about learning to speak louder than those voices.

let no unkind ideas take root in your mind.
that is a place where only flowers should grow.

— GARDENS

while we're here

how much money
we'd all save
(and corporations
would lose)
if we simply decided
we were our own
definition
of beautiful.

that we have nothing
yet to prove to them.

— DEFINITIONS

leeza jayde

it's peculiar,
i think,
that magazines
try to tell me
how i should
wear my own skin
when i was not born
with crossed legs,
and hairless arms,
and cherry lips.

— IT'S PECULIAR

while we're here

your body is a map
of every story
you've ever told.
every birthmark,
scar,
wrinkle
      —an artefact.

fossils in living skin.

yet more evidence
that you
have lived.

— EVIDENCE

leeza jayde

repeat after me:

i will let no hearth
contain my fire.

i will let no cage
ensnare my wings.

i will let no glass ceiling
strap my spirit down.

— MY MORNING MANTRA

while we're here

i was never a princess.
and i didn't need saving.

because i was the knight,
and i was the dragon
in my story.

let's be clear:

i saved myself
      from myself.

and i never needed
a boy to do that.

all i needed,
all i ever needed,
was the blade in my mouth
that God gifted me
and my fists,

and a pen.

— ALL I NEEDED

leeza jayde

teach yourself
to be someone,
when all they tell you
is to be someone's.

— YOU DON'T NEED SOMEBODY TO LOVE.

IT'S A PRIVILEGE. NOT A MUST.

while we're here

it is absurd
to paint women
as delicate.
no body that can
bleed and not die;
birth life through pain;
endure whistling,
wide-spread belittlement,
and media bombardments
about how they can always,
always improve
will ever be *weak*
in any sensible
definition of the word.

— THINK AGAIN

leeza jayde

if i should have a son one day,
i will raise him to know
that to cry, to struggle,
to talk about the maelstrom of thoughts
whirling around in his brain
is to be human.

human.

— AND NOTHING LESS

while we're here

it's your skin.
not theirs.
don't let them
ever tell you
how to wear it.

— YOUR SKIN

leeza jayde

WE ARE BORN,

then manufactured

while we're here

i danced
on the doorstep
of o b l i v i o n ,
and walked away
with the light
of a thousand
milky ways
in my eyes.

— I TRAVERSED THE UNIVERSE

                    AND CAME BACK TO MYSELF

leeza jayde

you deserve someone
who will help you
with opening
that overflowing
jar of dreams
you have hidden
behind your breast.

— WORDS OF AFFIRMATION

while we're here

i could see the beauty
in everyone
and everything
except for me.

— MY HOW TIMES HAVE CHANGED

leeza jayde

i wonder,

if you had to choose between
        growth
                or comfort,
what would matter most to you?

— WHAT SERVES YOU BETTER?

while we're here

here is my goodbye list:

three loves,
too many important family members,
and my own self-loathing.

— SOME OF THESE I MISS MORE THAN OTHERS

leeza jayde

i sling my rucksack over the chair,
wipe the blood from my lip,
the war paint from my eyes.

'it's over,' i say.

                'it's finally over.'

i won the war.

maybe not forever,

      but for now.

— AND THAT IS ENOUGH

while we're here

you flood my soul
with the gentlest sunshine
i have honestly ever known.

— A SHORT LETTER TO MY FRIENDS

leeza jayde

i have grown to love
the way people pass notes
back
    and
forth
using only their eyes
and silent smiles.

— TO AND FRO

while we're here

you make me think about death.

not in a morbid way.
just that life is momentary
and that songs end,
and suns collapse, and flowers die

    but that while they're here,
they are loud, and warm, and *bright*.

yes. you make me think about death

    and that while we're alive,

        we should live.

— ARE YOU BREATHING
                OR LIVING?

leeza jayde

fresh sheets and thunder
outside my rattling window,
cocooned in a blanket
my nanna knitted me when i was seven,
sipping my mug of milkless tea
lovingly holding a tattered paperback.

this is what they tell you about
when you're a child.

it just looks different with adult eyes.

this is it though.

this is what magic feels like.

— SLOWING DOWN

while we're here

when i was nineteen
i had this
useless superpower.

i stepped on my own cape
and my thoughts were
a cruel kind of kryptonite.

i had a useless superpower
when i was nineteen.

leeza jayde

but now
i possess this
power
to weave words
out of all of my old
pain.

to exhale the dirt
and the ashes
and the soot
and birth kingdoms
with my pen.

and, i will admit,
that sometimes i still
fall quiet,
but my hand cramps
from everything i never said
and have yet to say.

i've gained a really useful superpower
since i was nineteen.

— WHEN I WAS NINETEEN, PART II

while we're here

life is beautiful
if only you know
where to look.

— EYES OPEN

leeza jayde

who is this
s m i l i n g f a c e
staring at me
in the mirror?

— IT'S NICE TO SEE YOU AGAIN,

        MY CHILDHOOD FRIEND

while we're here

if you crave
the taste
of happiness
then only pile your plate
with flavours that fill
your stomach
with joy.

— DON'T LET YOURSELF DOWN

leeza jayde

i find myself
always humming now.

it's as if my soul
is sharing
the new song
life has conducted
within me.

one i have learned
to compose
as i go.

— WINGING IT

while we're here

i pray that
one day
you won't need
to wear that
smiling mask
that you slip on
like a second skin
anymore.

— DAILY MASQUERADE

leeza jayde

while we're here

THE LIGHT LIVES

wherever you let it

leeza jayde

now i see
that i spent so long
fighting against a current
that was flowing me towards
cleaner waters.

and isn't that so typical of humans?

to resist change.

    to resist medicine.

— CLEANER WATERS

while we're here

i write poetry
because someone out there
has an emptiness
that maybe my words
can start to plant seeds in
and help better things grow,
just as other word weavers
have done for me.

i am simply paying it forward.

and if even just one poem,
one line, one word
can get them through the hour
while they themselves undergo
the hard work in healing
then i'll have done my job
as a fellow ~~poet~~ human being.

— WE ARE ALL IN THIS TOGETHER

leeza jayde

i never used to write in lowercases.

but all that changed
when i went through pain.

because now i want to whisper
harsh truths gently
because life will not always
be gentle with you

— BUT I'LL TRY TO BE

while we're here

i want to spread kindness
the way that dandelions spread their seeds.
softly. in waves that quietly ride the wind
and somehow end up landing
everywhere.

— IT LIVES IN YOU

leeza jayde

i saw you again today.

it's been three months since you died
and left all this laughter echoing in our empty house.
like an atomic bomb's aftermath, i see your silhouette
burned into the air in every room. and i was there
at your funeral and i cried then and most nights since

but today was different
        because i saw you again.

it left me breathless how alive and vibrant you looked.
there. right in front of me
        in a stranger's smile.

in the way they gently took the grocery bag i'd
  numbly packed
before turning off my checkout register
and wished me a better day with warmth in
  their voice.

i saw you on the bus ride home as well,
in the way someone gave up their seat for me
because i swayed like a skeletal tree
from too many sleepless nights.
in the way they helped me sit, and offered me
their last few sips of water.

while we're here

you were there when i came home to
my mother's open arms, and i heard your care
in 11 new voicemails from friends
who knew what you meant to me.

and it occurs to me now
        that you never really left.

that wherever kindness lives,
        you do too.

because you wrapped me in it, gifted it to me,
every day until you closed your eyes for good.

and that photos are not what
        keep you alive.

that what you stood for does.
        and always will.

— THOMAS

leeza jayde

i kind of like how time blurs together
when we are.

— EPHEMERAL

while we're here

'it's *weird*,' you say.

i look at you, our legs dangling over the cliff.
we're both still watching the starlight glitter
off the ocean's rolling, wet skin.
the moon hangs like a cat's eye,
winking in and out of white, wispy clouds.

'what is?' i ask.

'this,' you say. 'right here. now.'

i tell you i don't understand, and you smile.
you always smile when i don't understand something.

you close your eyes, and say, 'this is the oldest
    we've ever been, right here, *now*,
and the youngest we'll ever be again.'

i blink then, because it's true.
    and just like that, the moment is gone,
replaced by another moment we'll never get back.
    another *now*.

    and another.

— AND ANOTHER.
    AND ANOTHER.

THIS IS IT.

THIS IS HOW
a heart heals.

while we're here

your soul and skin
are the canvas.

what you go through in life
is the colour.

and your hands?

    well.

they hold
the paint brush.

leeza jayde

and what you do now

is entirely up to you.

while we're here

WE ARE BORN AS CANVASSES.

blank. ready to be stained with the many hues
that life has yet to paint us with.
and the world will indeed splatter you
with so many wondrous and strange
sweet, and bitter, shades.

you can choose to coat over the blue and greyscale tints
that speckle your skin
>—or you can decide to blend them into
> an entirely new colour.

BE MARKED—OR MARK YOURSELF.

> the choice is yours.

the beautiful thing about art is that
> it's open to interpretation.

regardless of what you'll do, it is inevitable that people,
and places, and experiences will paint you in unique ways.

but i genuinely hope that no matter what hues flow
through your veins, no matter how many creases your heart
folds itself into, or how much gold sluices through the cuts
in your kintsugi skin, that the colours you learn to bleed
will be ones bright and beautiful and bold
and unapologetically yourself.

leeza jayde

i hope many things for you,
but i hope for this most of all.

follow that compass behind your breast.
and do it all with that paintbrush between your fingers—
 between your teeth if you have to.

just live your life and let yourself make mistakes,
stretch, grow, learn. just do it all
 while you can.
do it all
 before you go.

do it all
 while we're here.

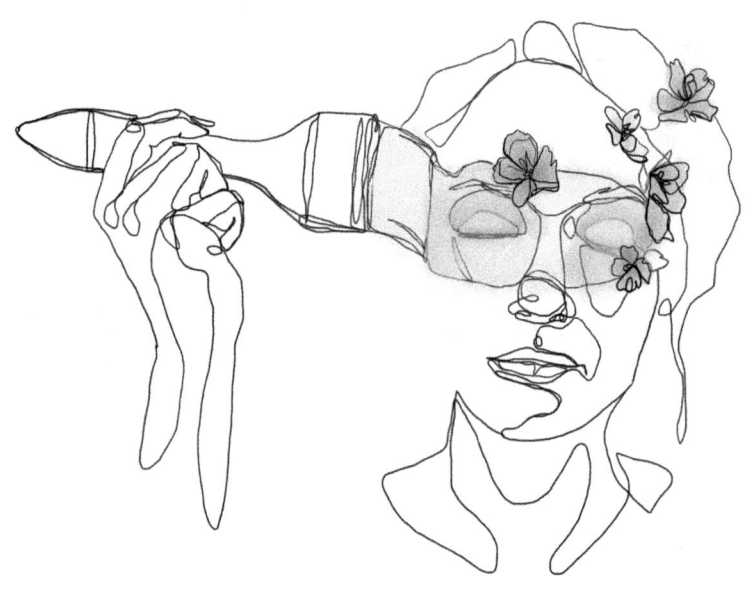

p.s.

thank you for reading
a thousand times,
             thank you.

ACKNOWLEDGEMENTS

it really does take a village.

for my mother. you tentatively mended these bones many times with that soothing magic you possess and share so selflessly.

for my father. you bandaged me in ink and held my little hands while i birthed kingdoms with my pen, ceaselessly murmuring encouragement.

for Patricia. nanna. you weaved dreams before my eyes. taught me to drink in moments. to garden, knit, laugh. to be mindful. to love.

for Ashley. my home.
thank you for believing in me.
for listening to my story.
for building a new one with me.

for my beloved Dale, Cara, Tiarnie, Shylee and Harry,
and my dearest Tyru, Kyle, Cass and Telle,
you fill me with a thousand suns and i would not have grown nearly as much these past few years without your unwavering support.
and to Sara, Hayden, Susan, Isabelle, Sarai, Peter, Chris, Jacob, Tabitha, Justin, Dave, Koomal, Caitlin, Holly, Katie, Luke, Les and Adelle.
your kindness thaws me. it always has.

for SK Williams. my dear Shayla and Kevin. i cannot thank you both enough for supporting my dream with your kindness and help.
you are two profoundly wonderful people and friends.

for my women wordsmiths.
to the beautiful Stellene, Shakira, Kristel, Chloe, Rukshaan, Steph, Olivia, Bella, Jenna.
you girls will move mountains. you've already begun to.

for Philipp and the emotive and poignant illustrations that you so carefully crafted to suit the messages splayed out on these pages.
(for more of Philipp's art, find him on instagram under @matterofline)

for Dianne.
my loving mentor, editor, friend.
you never really did stop believing in me, did you?

for Paige. thank you for your beautiful water colour edit of Philipp's art.

for me
and all the nights i stayed up
wondering, hurting, healing, sleepless.
writing. writing. writing.

for God.

the fight belongs to Him. and so does my heart.
you gifted me these words
so that i could gift them to others
and i owe you everything.

for my supportive, creative and uplifting instagram community.
what a journey it's been with you all.
thank you for every moment of your time.
without you, this book would not be in anybody's grasp
right now.

and for you, reader. i hope these word weavings find you well.
they are an accumulation of pocketed awakenings that i wrote through many sleepless nights, welcomed tears, countless smiles and throughout my travels.
so thank you for holding my dreams in your hands and
supporting them. i appreciate you visiting my mind.

even if it was just for a little while.

ABOUT THE AUTHOR

LEEZA JAYDE is a South Australian poet and young adult writer based in Adelaide. She is also an English and History high school teacher with an insatiable thirst for knowledge. When she isn't mouthing *help* from beneath a mountain of essays yet to be marked, she is also an animated creative writing workshop presenter, and an amateur astronomer who seeks adventure in every unexplored nook and cranny she can find.

You can find her on Instagram under @leezajaydepoetry, buried in tea-stained paperbacks or staring at the night sky, tracing constellations by the shoreline, with her feet clothed in sand.

- leezajaydepoetry
- leezajaydepoet
- leezajaydepoetry

www.ingramcontent.com/pod-product-compliance
Lightning Source LLC
Chambersburg PA
CBHW061321040426
42444CB00011B/2722